games people play!

United States

Philip Brooks

CHILDREN'S PRESS®
A Division of Grolier Publishing
New York • London • Hong Kong • Sydney
Danbury, Connecticut

Library of Congress Cataloging-in-Publication Data

Brooks, Philip, 1963–
United States / by Philip Brooks.
p. cm.—(Games people play)
Includes bibliographical references and index.
ISBN 0-516-04442-7
1. Sports—United States—Juvenile literature. 2. Games—United States—
Juvenile Literature. 3. Athletes—United States—Biography—Juvenile
literature. I. Title. II. Series.

GV583.B67 1996   95-49450
796'0973—dc20   CIP
                  AC

Editorial & Design Staff

Project Editor: Mark Friedman

Design and Electronic Composition:
  TJS Design

Cover Art and Icons: Susan Kwas

Activity Page Art: MacArt Design

Table of **C**ontents

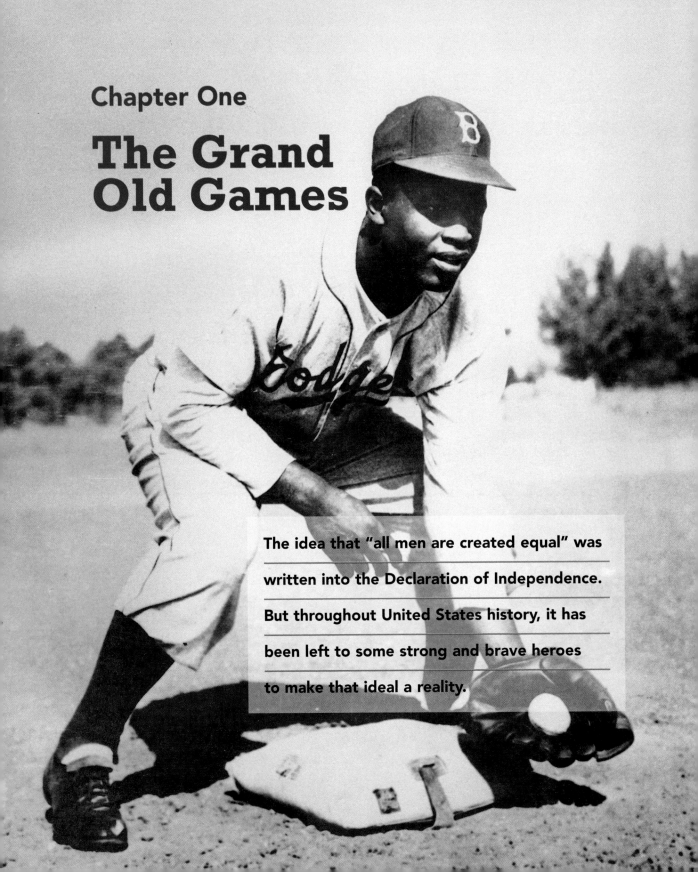

Chapter One
The Grand Old Games

The idea that "all men are created equal" was written into the Declaration of Independence. But throughout United States history, it has been left to some strong and brave heroes to make that ideal a reality.

During the summer of 1947, Jackie Robinson became one of these heroes simply by playing **baseball** for the Brooklyn Dodgers.

Jackie Robinson was the first African-American to play major-league baseball. It seems crazy to imagine today, but from the late 1800s to 1947, there were no players in the major leagues who were not Caucasian. A "gentleman's agreement" among major-league owners barred blacks from the game.

Before 1947, African-Americans, Latinos, and some American Indians played in the Negro Leagues. It may be argued that when Jackie Robinson first put on a Brooklyn Dodgers uniform, he launched the modern civil rights movement. That is how important sports and games are to people in the United States. Jackie Robinson stands tall in U.S. history because major-league baseball was, and is, vitally important to Americans. Baseball is not simply a game. It is part of daily life, history, and culture.

Above: Satchel Paige, one of the great stars of the Negro Leagues

Opposite Page:
Jackie Robinson

Alexander Cartwright

amateur

a person who performs a
service (or plays a sport)
without being paid

No one is certain how baseball came into existence. Most likely, it evolved in the 1800s from several older games, including the English game of rounders. For a long time, people believed that Abner Doubleday created baseball in Cooperstown, New York, in 1839. Today, historians believe this story to be mostly untrue. They credit Alexander Cartwright with molding the game into its present form. In 1845, Cartwright wrote a list of rules for his "base ball" club, the New York Knickerbockers. Many of Cartwright's rules are still in use today. For instance, Cartwright introduced the idea of tagging a runner out. Before then, fielders struck a runner with a thrown ball to record an out.

Baseball spread across the United States during and after the Civil War (1861–65). Soon after the war, baseball teams and amateur leagues began appearing everywhere. In 1869, the Cincinnati Red Stockings became the first team of professional, paid baseball players. In 1876, the National League was formed. The same professional league exists today, along with the American League (which was born in 1901). By the turn of the century, baseball was the most popular team sport in the United States.

Although baseball was the most popular sport, most Americans did not pay attention to the game. Professional athletes were looked down upon because they were mostly uneducated, ill-mannered, drinking men. In the 1920s, baseball was the first sport to be embraced by a vast majority of Americans. Historians credit one man with this revolution: Babe Ruth.

Until the 1920s, home runs were a rare occurrence in baseball. Pitchers such as Christy Mathewson and Cy Young dominated games, and scores were usually very low. The best home-run hitters collected between 10 and 15 homers a season. But in 1920, Babe Ruth joined the New York Yankees and began launching dozens of home runs a year. In 1927, he smashed an incredible 60 home runs, a record that was not broken for more than three decades.

Prisoners in a northern Civil War camp playing baseball

Babe Ruth was perhaps the most famous athlete in the history of American sports.

Babe Ruth had a personality to match his mighty bat. He was a large, imposing man with a jolly laugh and a happy face. He was the most famous athlete of his day, and perhaps the most famous person in the United States. Given the Yankees' success with Ruth, other teams began developing home-run hitters to draw in large crowds. With the excitement of high scores and frequent home runs, baseball gained fans by the millions every year. The sport's "golden age" extended from the 1920s to the 1960s. In that period, baseball was the "national pastime" of the United States. In the 1950s, baseball became one of the very first events shown on television, a new medium that would soon overtake radio. With the advent of nationally televised games, the World Series (baseball's annual championship series) became an October ritual that Americans cherished as much as Thanksgiving in November.

Baseball has endured trouble in recent decades. Beginning in the 1970s, baseball teams began making tremendous profits from television broadcasts. In turn, players began earning millions of dollars a year. Despite so much money being made, owners and players have fought bitterly over money. In 1994, a players' strike forced the cancellation of the World Series. It was the first time the Series was not played since 1904.

Some fans have given up on baseball because of these problems. But tens of millions still attend games at major- and minor-league ballparks each year. Even more watch the game on cable and network television. Major-league teams are beginning to promote the game on the Internet, as well. Variations of the game are played on sandlots and urban streets across the country. Despite the game's troubles, millions of American children still dream of being a hero in October's World Series.

Sandy Koufax, a pitching great in the 1960s

Millions of boys and girls play Little League baseball. The best teams from around the world compete in the Little League World Series, which is held every August in Williamsport, Pennsylvania.

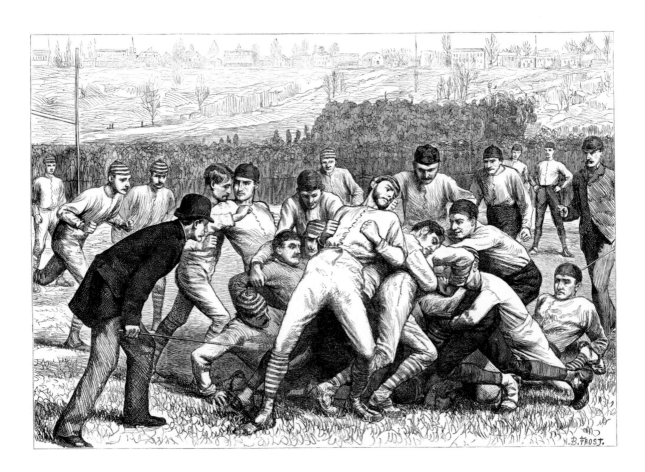

A football match between Yale and Princeton in the 1870s, when football still resembled rugby

The World Series is still a big event in the life of the United States. But Super Bowl Sunday is almost a national holiday. Virtually the entire country sits down for an evening in January to watch football's championship game.

Football combines rugby's running, tackling, and passing with soccer's kicking. The earliest recorded game took place in 1869 between Princeton and Rutgers universities. But this game looked nothing like a modern football game. There were 25 players on each side instead of today's 11. Rules were more like those used in soccer.

In 1880, a man named Walter Camp introduced some of the modern rules that are more familiar to today's fans. His rules called for 11 players on a side and created the dominant role for the quarterback. He also invented football's complicated system of measuring yardage and downs.

quarterback
the most important player on a football team; calls plays, throws passes, hands off the ball

Early football, played with little padding and only makeshift helmets without face masks, was even more violent and dangerous than today's game. In the early 1900s, the game was marred by serious injuries and several deaths. President Theodore Roosevelt called for changes in the rules to make football safer. One such change was the elimination of all blocking with extended arms. This avoided broken noses, gouged eyes, and cracked jawbones.

Soon, football became popular in colleges. In 1910, the National Collegiate Athletic Association (NCAA) was formed to govern college football's championship games, called "bowl" games. In this era, the Rose Bowl, Cotton Bowl, and Orange Bowl became some of the biggest sports events in the country.

The National Football League (NFL) was formed in 1922. The league struggled for national attention in its early years, but then it gained many fans when its games were broadcast on television in the 1950s. In 1959, a rival league was formed — the American Football League (AFL). The two leagues competed for seven years until they were merged in 1966. In the new alignment, the NFL was divided into two conferences, the National Football Conference (NFC) and the American Football Conference (AFC). The same arrangement exists today, and every season, the two conference champions meet in the Super Bowl.

High-school football also is enormously popular throughout the United States. In many small towns, the games are taken as seriously as professional games. Texas, especially, is known for taking its football wins and losses to heart. High-school football heroes sometimes remain local heroes for life.

Running back Emmitt Smith
(#22) of the Dallas Cowboys

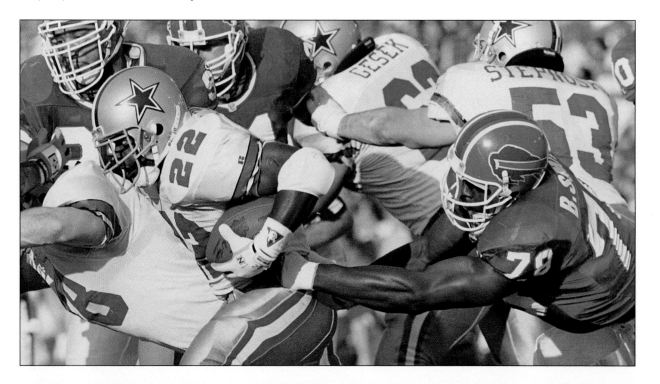

If football and baseball are games of wide-open spaces, **basketball** belongs to cramped gymnasiums and playgrounds. Basketball is played everywhere in the United States — suburban driveways, country backyards, and city playgrounds. The game is perhaps best-loved by inner-city kids. Because they do not have access to the grass fields and open space that baseball and football demand, city kids turn to basketball. The game requires little more than a ball and a hoop.

Many young people in poor neighborhoods dream of making millions of dollars in the NBA. But there are fewer than 500 players in the NBA, and there are thousands of good players who never make it. Many NBA players encourage young basketball players to pursue their education and not pin all their hopes on basketball. Basketball should be a way to have fun and stay healthy.

Michael Jordan is the greatest basketball player alive. He rose to fame by soaring through the air and dunking the ball with his tongue sticking out.

Did you know that when basketball was invented, nobody dunked? In basketball's early days, players were not allowed to take jump shots or even to dribble the basketball.

James Naismith, a physical education teacher at a YMCA in Springfield, Massachusetts, invented the game in 1891. He intended it as a variation on rugby that could be played indoors when the weather turned cold.

In the original basketball game, players passed the ball to each other while standing still, and each team tried to throw the ball into a peach basket hung on the wall. Very few baskets (called "field goals") were scored in the early game. It was several years before the basket's bottom was cut out. Until then, the game had to stop while someone retrieved the ball after each goal.

Basketball spread quickly throughout the Northeast, and the first professional game was played in 1896. But in the sport's first decades, basketball games remained slow, plodding struggles. Many games ended in all-out brawls because players attempted to steal the ball by tackling the player who held it. In the 1920s, the faster, higher-scoring college game grew in popularity, and for years, college basketball overshadowed the pro game.

Left: To keep the ball in play, a large cage was built around many basketball courts in the early 20th century. Because of this cage, basketball players were long known as "cagers."

Right: This 1892 photo shows basketball being played with a basket that still had its bottom.

In the 1990s, women's college basketball has gained popularity at a dramatic rate. The NCAA championship game is the most popular women's collegiate sports event in the country.

The National Basketball Association (NBA) was formed in 1949 after the merger of two smaller leagues. The first dominant team in the NBA was the Minneapolis Lakers, led by the mighty George Mikan. At 6-foot-10, Mikan was the first big man to star in pro basketball. Basketball's most legendary dynasty remains the Boston Celtics of the 1950s and 1960s. Coached by Red Auerbach, the Celtics won eight NBA championships from 1958 to 1965.

The American Basketball Association (ABA) was formed in 1967 as a rival to the NBA. The ABA played a faster-paced and flashier style of basketball than the NBA. When the ABA went out of business in 1976, some of its teams joined the NBA. Beginning with this merger, the NBA began to gain momentum. In the early 1980s, Earvin "Magic" Johnson and Larry Bird entered the NBA. Either Johnson's Los Angeles Lakers or Bird's Boston Celtics won 8 of the 9 NBA championships from 1980 to 1988 and captured the hearts of American sports fans. With the arrival of Michael Jordan in 1984, pro basketball began attracting fans who had never watched sports at all. Jordan earned acclaim as the greatest

basketball player ever — perhaps the greatest athlete ever. Many fans believe that basketball has surpassed baseball and football as the most popular pro sport in the United States. Men's and women's basketball is played and watched with passion in colleges and high schools. In Europe and the Middle East, several highly successful basketball leagues have been formed. And all of this began with some young men throwing balls into peach baskets in a YMCA gym about a century ago.

Wilt Scores 100

Wilt Chamberlain was the biggest, strongest center in the 1960s. The 7-foot-1 Philadelphia Warrior holds a record that nobody else has matched: he scored 100 points in a single game. On March 2, 1962, "Wilt the Stilt" made just about every shot and dunk he tried. With 46 seconds left on the clock, teammate Joe Rucklick pulled down a defensive rebound and fired the ball downcourt to Chamberlain, who was standing beneath his own basket. Wilt jammed it home for his 99th and 100th points of the game.

More than 30 years later, Wilt's record is intact. Not only did he set the record, he owns six of the ten highest-scoring games in NBA history. In separate games, Chamberlain scored 100, 78, 73 (twice), 72, 70, and 68 points. Since Wilt scored 100 in 1962, the closest anyone has come was David Thompson, who scored 73 on April 9, 1978. And today's best scorer, Michael Jordan, has gone only as high as 69.

How Do I Play Basketball?

A Hoops Glossary

More than any other American game, basketball has developed a life of its own on the street, on playgrounds, in backyards, and in alleys. As this "street ball" has grown, an original vocabulary of basketball terms also has developed.

Here is a sample of some of these terms:

board ⊕ rebound

crossover ⊕ to dribble the ball from one hand to the other intending to deceive a defender

cut (as in *cut to the hole*) ⊕ to run toward the basket without the ball, hoping to receive a pass

drive ⊕ to run toward the basket while dribbling the ball

dunk (also **jam; slam; stuff**) ⊕ to forcefully throw the ball through the basket for a field goal

fast break ⊕ when a defensive team steals the ball and quickly runs (or *breaks*) toward the basket

glass ⊕ the backboard (which is often made of Plexiglas)

hoop (also **bucket; hole; rim**) ⊕ a basket or field goal, as in *to score a hoop*

hoops ⊕ the game of basketball itself, as in *to play some hoops*

in your face ⊕ to have a dunk scored against you

kick out ⊕ to dribble toward the basket and suddenly pass the ball to an outside shooter

paint ⊕ the foul lane (the painted area on the court)

rejection ⊕ a blocked shot

'sister ⊕ an assist; a pass that leads directly to a field goal or a dunk

three (also **downtown; trey**) ⊕ a three-point basket, as in *shoot a three*

The Players

Basketball is played by two teams of five players; teams carry about ten additional reserves, who sit on the bench during most of the game. A *center,* usually the team's tallest player, stays under the basket most of the time. On offense, the center tries to get the ball for an easy layup or a dunk. On defense, the center collects rebounds and tries to block shots. A *forward* is a tall player who plays mostly near the baseline to be in position for rebounds. On offense, forwards often run in circular patterns to get in position for passes from teammates. *Guards* are usually the shortest and fastest players on the team. They usually stay back between the free-throw line and the center line and take outside shots. A team's five players on the court usually consist of one center, two forwards, and two guards.

The Court

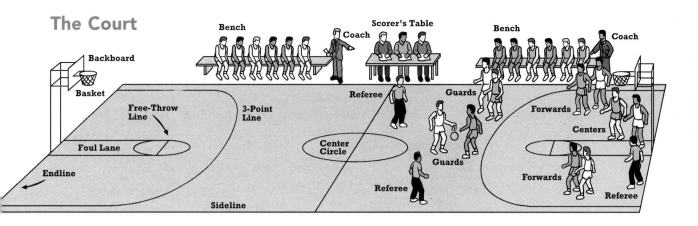

Bench · Coach · Scorer's Table · Bench · Coach · Backboard · Basket · Free-Throw Line · 3-Point Line · Referee · Guards · Forwards · Centers · Foul Lane · Center Circle · Guards · Forwards · Endline · Referee · Referee · Sideline

The Game

A basketball game begins at center court with a *jump ball* — a referee throws the ball in the air, and the teams' two centers jump and try to tap the ball to their teammates. The team that recovers the ball is on offense first; the other team is on defense. On offense, a team must shoot for a basket before the *shot clock* runs out (the NBA shot clock is 24 seconds; in college and high school it is 45 seconds). Offensive players can score by throwing the ball through the basket. Players can score a two-point *field goal* (any shot taken from the floor, or a dunk); a three-point field goal (a shot taken from behind the three-point line); or a one-point *free throw* (a shot taken at the free-throw line). Free throws are awarded to an offensive player who has been *fouled* (hit or bumped) by a defensive player. If a player's field-goal shot misses the basket, all the players scramble for possession of the *loose ball*. When a field goal or free throw is made, the ball is turned over to the other team, which then goes on offense.

Kids play basketball anywhere, even if a full court and a gym aren't available.

Baseball, basketball, and football are the most popular professional sports in the United States. But none of these is the most popular game in the world. **Soccer** is the world's most-played, most-watched sport. It is enjoyed by billions of people! In fact, the United States is one of the few countries where soccer is not the national game. That may change in the near future. Today, more kids play in soccer leagues than any other sport. Several professional leagues have been established and failed in the United States, but the game flourishes on the high school and college levels.

Why do U.S. fans prefer other sports to soccer? The major reason seems to be the game's low scoring. Many soccer matches end in scores of 1–0 or 2–1. In basketball, by contrast, there is virtually nonstop scoring, with teams breaking 100 points in most games. In American football, there are usually several touchdowns per game, and scores range from the teens to the forties. It seems that U.S. fans are not accustomed to the defensive struggles of soccer.

American football

the version of football invented in America that involves tackling; "football" is the more common name for "soccer" around the world

Millions of American girls and boys love playing soccer.

Alexi Lalas, star of the 1994 U.S. national soccer team

In 1994, the United States hosted the World Cup, the world's championship soccer tournament. Teams from 24 different nations came to the United States to compete. Before the tournament, some people predicted that Americans would not show much interest in the games. They were wrong. More than 3.5 million people came to see the tournament, an attendance total that broke the previous World Cup record by more than a million. Inspired by hometown support, the U.S. national team surprised everyone by advancing deep into the tournament. It was eliminated by the powerhouse team from Brazil, but after the game, the crowd cheered the U.S. players as if they were winners.

In cold-weather spots such as Minnesota and upper New England, **hockey** helps makes winter bearable. The game was brought to Canada by British soldiers stationed there in the 1860s.

It quickly spread south. Professional hockey came to the United States in 1924, when the Boston Bruins became the first U.S. team in Canada's National Hockey League (NHL). The NHL now has teams throughout the United States, even as far south as Florida, where an ice rink is only an indoor occurrence.

Wayne Gretzky, perhaps the greatest hockey player ever, played several seasons for the Los Angeles Kings.

NHL hockey has long been known as the roughest professional sport, and games are often marred by bench-clearing fights. A much cleaner level of play exists in colleges and minor leagues. Perhaps because the puck is too small to be seen well on television, hockey has never been a major television sport. This may have held down its popularity, but also probably helps maintain the sport's gritty tradition. Other sports have changed to accommodate television, but hockey has not.

Across the United States, young people and adults love to play a variety of other team sports. Field hockey, volleyball, softball, and water polo are staples of college athletics. **Rugby** also is turning into a popular pastime. The game is a combination of football and soccer. The ball is shaped like a football, though a bit larger. As in football, players run, pass and kick the ball in an effort to advance past the goal line. The defense tries to tackle the ball carrier before he or she can do so. The game is more like soccer in that the action is continuous. When a player is stopped, he or she tries to pass or kick the ball forward. Rugby is the only full-contact sport played widely among U.S. women.

The New Jersey Devils won the Stanley Cup (the NHL's championship tournament) in 1995.

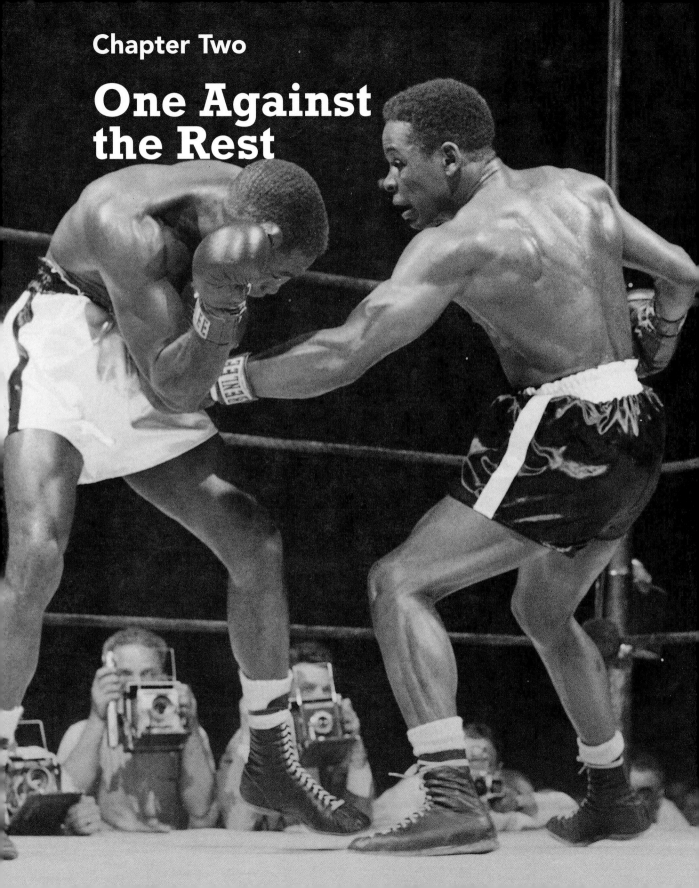

Chapter Two

One Against the Rest

I n American culture, people love stories that depict the victory of underdogs — individuals fighting their way to the top against more powerful opponents. Perhaps that explains the continuing popularity of sports that pit one person against another. One such sport is **boxing**.

During the 1950s, boxing was the second-most-popular spectator sport in the United States (only baseball was more popular). Television brought the fights into people's homes every Friday night. Everyone knew the name of the current champions. Today, boxing is a flashy, multimillion-dollar industry. The biggest prizefights are carried on pay-per-view television, and fighters earn millions per bout — whether they win or lose!

Boxers earn big money because they must endure months of training for a single fight and because the risks of their sport are so high. In training, boxers run many miles, skip rope, and work out with punching bags hour after hour. Also, they must learn fighting tactics and strategies by sparring. Sparring is a practice fight with an opponent who does not attempt to win. When a boxer makes a mistake, the penalty is usually a vicious punch. The hits can be so hard that a single blow can end one's life.

Muhammad Ali was perhaps the greatest boxer of all time. He was extremely intelligent both in and out of the ring. Ali's motto was "float like a butterfly, sting like a bee." He did just that. In a fight, Ali was both graceful and powerful, moving on feet as quick as a dancer's. In his long career, Ali also caused controversy. In the 1960s, he changed his name from Cassius Clay to Muhammad Ali. This was based on his Muslim beliefs. He believed that Cassius Clay was his "slave name" assigned by white society. Later, Ali was drafted into the U.S. military to fight in the Vietnam War, but he refused to go. He claimed that his religious beliefs prevented him from killing people. Ali was stripped of his boxing title and went to jail. Many people called him a coward. Today, most people look upon his stand against the Vietnam War as heroic.

Young people interested in boxing can compete in Golden Gloves competitions. Here, fights consist of three rounds of three minutes each. Most of the great fighters began their careers in such amateur competitions. The Olympics also have been a launching pad to fame. "Sugar" Ray Leonard and George Foreman are just two Olympic medalists who went on to great careers in the pro ring.

In recent years, boxing has been criticized as a dangerous sport that should be banned. Some critics say that boxers should wear protective helmets, which would decrease the risk of head injuries.

Boxing places two competitors in a bloody and dangerous one-on-one fight. Similar intensity (without the violence) is present in other sports pitting individuals against one another. Tennis and golf are two such sports that are widely popular in the United States.

Muhammad Ali shouts at Sonny Liston after knocking him out in 1969.

Tennis was invented in France in about A.D. 1200, and it arrived in the United States in the 1870s. Since its beginnings, tennis was a sport enjoyed by European royalty and the well-to-do. It was thought of as a quiet game with strict rules. Players wore white clothes and behaved politely.

Venus Williams, a U.S. tennis star on the rise

In the United States, tennis changed in the 1970s. American tennis stars such as Jimmy Connors and John McEnroe began winning championships. They brought a new, aggressive attitude to the tennis court. At the same time, women's tennis was gaining popularity as such American stars as Billie Jean King, Chris Evert, and Martina Navratilova (who defected to the United States from Czechoslovakia) began to dominate the world.

With American players dominating tennis, the sport entered a period of booming popularity in the United States. Tennis courts were built in communities everywhere in the 1970s. Amateur players waited hours for courts to open. Today, however, Americans have cooled a bit to the sport. People have moved on to a variety of other fitness sports, such as swimming, squash, aerobics, and weight lifting. Fewer people are playing tennis in everyday life, but the United States is still turning out world-championship players. Pete Sampras and Andre Agassi have been among the dominant players in world tennis for most of the 1990s.

By the time he was three years old, Eldrick "Tiger" Woods could beat any ten-year-old golfer he played. By age six, he already had made two holes in one. When he was 11, Tiger was undefeated during a full year of California Junior Golf. He played in 30 tournaments, and he won them all!

In 1994, at age 18, Tiger became the youngest man ever to win the U.S. Amateur Open. He was also the first African-American to win the tournament (Tiger is also part American Indian, Chinese, Thai, and Caucasian). In 1995, Woods repeated the championship.

Tiger appeared as an amateur in the 1995 U.S. Open. Before the tournament, a reporter told Tiger that he was a 100-to-1 shot to win. Tiger burst out laughing, and the reporter asked Tiger what he thought the odds should be. Woods said, "Against those guys? How about maybe a million to one!"

As a young pro golfer, the odds are still against Tiger. But it won't be long before he is a golf champion.

Golf, which originated in Scotland, came to the United States in the 1800s. The first U.S. golfing club was established in Yonkers, New York, in 1888. A man named John Reid created a nine-hole course in an apple orchard there.

Golf has come a long way in the United States since that first nine-hole course. Today, lush green golf courses are spread over acres of land in virtually every American county. Even where there isn't enough room for a full 18-hole course, driving ranges are built so that people can practice their swings. In downtown Chicago, a golf course exists on a large city block surrounded by skyscrapers.

To be a golfer with the best equipment, a person could spend thousands of dollars on golf clubs, shoes, clothes, balls, and a golf cart. And then, one must pay for time to play on a golf course. Or, a person must join a country club with its own course. Some country clubs are quite expensive, and many refuse to admit certain people who apply for membership. Several of the most exclusive clubs in the United States traditionally have not allowed memberships to African-Americans, Jewish people, and women.

For the most part, such discrimination is a thing of the past. But still, court battles are being fought to force several private clubs to integrate their membership.

Bobby Jones became the first American golfer to excel professionally. He dominated the game during the 1920s. Perhaps the most legendary American golfer was Mildred "Babe" Didrikson Zaharias. Golf, however was only one of Babe Didrikson's sports. She established herself as a superb athlete in the Olympics in the 1930s. A decade later, she turned to golf. In 1946 and 1947, she won 17 amateur golf tournaments in a row. After becoming a professional in 1948, she continued her incredible dominance. In her first four years as a pro, she won 24 major pro tournaments and finished second in 15 others. She won the Women's U.S. Open three times. The third time, in 1954, she was recovering from an operation to fight the cancer that eventually took her life in 1956. Boosted by the throngs of people who came to watch her play, Didrikson helped establish the Ladies Professional Golf Association (LPGA) in 1948. The same association organizes the major women's golf tournaments today.

Babe Didrikson Zaharias is still considered the greatest woman athlete in American sports history.

Chapter Three

Humans Against Nature

People in ancient cultures did not climb mountains for fun. They wanted to map the surrounding geography, or to find out if gods lived among the clouds. Today, we can map the world from satellites, so we do not have any real need to climb mountains. But many Americans test themselves against the mammoth power of mountains just for fun.

Mountaineering is a test of endurance, concentration, courage, and strength. Mistakes can be deadly. There are three distinct types of climbing: rock climbing, snow and ice climbing, and mixed mountaineering.

Rock climbers use rope, special spikes called pitons, and snap links to attach ropes to the pitons. Rock climbers make their way up a cliff that is almost vertical. They pull themselves up by clinging to crevices and outcroppings of rock. They must place their hands and feet carefully and move efficiently. Professional rock climbers can make incredible inverted (upside down) climbs over sheer granite using only their fingertips, toes, and superior body control.

Snow and ice climbing take place mostly at high elevations, where it is cold all the time. Climbers attach spikes called crampons to their boots. They use ice hammers, axes, and special pitons designed to screw into hard ice. Such climbers need not only strength and endurance, but a superior knowledge of snow and ice conditions. They must be able to spot impending avalanches or melting ice in order to stay alive.

Above: Ice climbing places climbers in freezing and dangerous positions.

Opposite page: Rock climbers need a sure grip to survive their sport.

Mixed mountaineering demands skills from both regular climbing and snow and ice climbing. One needs to be an accomplished mixed climber before attempting to climb major U.S. peaks, such as Mount McKinley in Alaska or Mount Ranier in Washington.

Many climbers train indoors on specially designed walls. Recreation clubs featuring these artificial rock faces are becoming more and more popular. They provide a safe climbing environment, even for children.

At least mountains don't move while you climb them. Many Americans love the challenge of conquering the water — on a boat, or a surfboard, or with no more equipment than a swimsuit. **Sailing** is a sport that provides the participants a certain amount of protection from the elements. The skill of sailing lies in steering a boat on open water and through ever-changing winds.

Sailing may seem like a peaceful sport, but it can be dangerous. Sailors must understand wind and weather patterns and must anticipate the reactions of their boat to the conditions. Storms on the ocean

A kayaker shoots the rapids.

can be more extreme than those on land, and they can surround a boat with little warning.

Kayaking is another popular boating sport. A kayak is a descendant of the canoe, a type of boat developed by American Indians centuries ago. The modern kayak is a short, narrow boat almost like a hollow surfboard. There is an opening in the top just large enough to hold a seated person. There also are double kayaks, long enough for two people. Kayakers love rivers with rapids, where the fast-moving whitewater sends them on a roller-coaster ride. On more difficult rivers and streams, kayakers need great maneuvering skill to avoid crashing into the rocks.

Kayaking can be defined as a **thrill sport**. Many athletes are not satisfied with riding a bike on a flat road, or swimming laps in a pool. The most daring athletes want to push themselves to faster, more dangerous challenges.

Bungee jumping is perhaps the most controversial of all thrill sports. A bungee cord is a heavy-duty length of elastic rope. One end of the cord is anchored to a bridge or the end of a construction crane; the other is attached to the jumper's ankles. The jumper leaps and falls through space for several seconds until the bungee cord runs out. At the bottom of the fall, the bungee yanks the jumper back up. Several people have been seriously injured when their bungee cords have snapped.

Sky diving is a sport that developed out of the World War II practice of soldiers parachuting into enemy territory from airplanes. Thrill seekers now pay money to ride in airplanes only to jump out and sail to the ground with a parachute. Today, simple sky diving cannot compare to the thrill of **sky surfing**. In this variation, jumpers leave the safety of the airplane with a modified surfboard attached to their feet. The board creates wind resistance, which a skilled sky surfer can use to perform incredible flips, rolls, and turns while falling at speeds over 100 miles per hour!

Not all thrill sports take place in the air. In 1994, an estimated 19 million people were **in-line skaters**. In-line skates are a variation of old-fashioned roller skates. Roller skates had four wheels set like the wheels of a car, while in-line

Bungee jumping

Sky surfing

wheels are set in a parallel row. This allows more speed and better steering. The skates were invented in 1980 as a way for Minnesota ice skaters to practice in the summer. Today, the skates are used for all sorts of activities, from simple aerobic exercise to thrilling tricks. So-called "extreme" skaters use special skates to fly down steep hills at high speed. "Aggressive" skaters perform dangerous tricks such as skating down stairs backwards or leaping from ramps. Most skaters wear a helmet, gloves, and elbow and knee pads to protect against serious injury.

Skateboarders, much like in-line skaters, have various reasons for taking up their hobby. Most kids skateboard for fun, but there are professionals who perform incredible tricks. Some use the concrete fixtures they find in their neighborhoods (such as museum steps, railings, or park benches), while others construct special ramps to show their stuff.

In-line skating

Not all thrill sports involve high-tech equipment and falling out of the sky. A truly American tradition that is more than a century old is the **rodeo**. The many events involved in the rodeo (pronounced either ROH-dee-oh or ro-DAY-oh) date back to the 1800s, when easterners flocked to the wide-open West. Ranching became a major industry, as cattle, horses, and sheep were raised, rounded up, sold, and transported by train to regions across North America.

The rodeo is really a collection of chores performed by cowboys in the Old West. Ranchers needed to tie hogs to bring them to slaughter. Cowboys rode bucking horses to tame them for riding. The first known official rodeo (with prizes and paying spectators) took place in 1888 in Prescott, Arizona. Today, rodeos are held throughout the United States. Many take place indoors at huge city arenas. But the sport is most popular in the West, where ranching is still a thriving industry and real cowboys still ride the range. To people unfamiliar with the rodeo, it might appear cruel to the animals involved. But the American Humane Society strictly enforces rules concerning their care. Most of these rules are unnecessary because owners of valuable livestock do not want their animals to be hurt.

rancher

a person who own or works on a ranch, which is a farm for raising horses or cattle

There are two types of events in the modern rodeo. Rough stock events are those in which cowboys ride bucking broncos or bulls for a specified number of seconds, usually eight. Points are awarded based on riding form and on how thoroughly riders spur the animal. Timed events include hog-tying and steer-wrestling. Points are awarded based on how quickly the task is completed.

Traditionally, women have been allowed to participate only in the barrel-racing event, but this is changing. In barrel racing, cowgirls race on horseback through a twisting race course made up of barrels. For greater speed, riders turn as close to the barrels as possible without knocking them over.

Riding a bucking bronco is one of the most exciting events at a rodeo.

Chapter Four
Racing!

It begins as a far-off whine. You can see the cars coming — bits of color gliding along the track. Then, suddenly, they are only a few feet away. Their engines blare like jet planes. The cars zoom past so quickly that their colors blur before your eyes. This is the Indianapolis 500.

T he Indy 500 (as it is called) is the biggest **auto racing** event in the United States. Crowds in excess of 300,000 jam the speedway's stands and infield (the vast area in the center of the track). It is almost impossible to see the cars from the infield, but nobody seems to care. These fans are just thrilled to be there.

Indy cars are specially designed for racing on an oval track with high, banked turns. The cars have wide, sticky tires to increase traction on the track. Front and rear wings produce "downforce." This means that air pressure forces the car downward rather than allowing it to fly out of control. Indy cars run on methanol rather than gasoline. Burning methanol creates less heat than gasoline. This allows the engine to crank up to 200 miles (320 km) per hour with less danger of the engine overheating and catching fire. Using methanol also reduces the risk of fire in case of a crash. All these precautions make Indy a surprisingly safe race.

A sleek Indy car, which is designed to cut through wind resistance and reach death-defying speeds

Indy car racing is not the only type of auto racing in the United States. **Stock car racing** is the most popular form of the sport, especially in southern states. Indy cars are built somewhat like airplanes, but stock car racing uses automobile models similar to the cars your family drives. Stock cars may look like the family sedan, but under the hood, they have specially built engines to make them fly. The National Association for Stock Car Auto Racing (NASCAR) allows only American-made cars to race in official events.

Drag racing features pure, blazing speed. Dragsters are like rockets on wheels, built to

Richard Petty (above) is perhaps the greatest stock car driver in the history of the sport. In a career that stretched from the 1960s to the 1990s, Petty won the Daytona 500 (stock car racing's biggest race) a record seven times.

In drag racing, cars start off with an explosive burst of speed.

You do not need a driver's license to enter the Soap Box Derby. Anyone between ages 9 and 16 is eligible. Contestants from across the nation build small, motor-less cars and race them on special downhill tracks.

In the past, the cars were built out of wooden crates made to carry soap. That is how the race got its name. Today, many of the cars are built with aluminum and graphite bodies. They are shaped to slice through the air and gain momentum as they coast down a long, straight track. Cars can be no longer than 80 inches (203 cm), and they must weigh 250 pounds (113 kg) or less. Most cost between $200 and $2,000 to build. Parents often help with construction of the cars. Qualifying races are held throughout the country every summer. The winners from every region of the country meet each August at the All-American Soap Box Derby in Akron, Ohio.

travel one quarter of a mile, as fast as possible. The cars are long and narrow, with huge, fat tires in the rear and small tires in front. They blast straight ahead at 200 miles an hour or faster. As soon as they cross the finish line, drivers deploy special parachutes to bring the cars to a stop.

American hobbyists have been known to "soup up" their engines. Using special parts, they turn their ordinary cars into **hot rods**. Many of these modifications may make a car illegal to drive on the street. Though it is illegal, amateur drag racing continues, especially in rural areas. Any time two owners argue over whose "ride" is faster, there is danger of a race. People often are killed when something goes wrong in such races. Auto racing is better left to the likes of Indy greats Al Unser and A. J. Foyt, or NASCAR heroes Cale Yarborough and Dale Earnhardt.

Secretariat

Everyone agreed that Secretariat was beautiful. In fact, his trainer said, "He might be too pretty to be a good horse." Secretariat grew up to be big and powerful, but he remained gentle, calm, and sure of himself. People who had seen a lot of horses believed he had the personality of a champion. They were right. In 1973, he won the Triple Crown, setting time records at the Kentucky Derby and Belmont Stakes.

After winning the Triple Crown in such convincing fashion, Secretariat (below right) made the covers of *Time, Newsweek,* and *Sports Illustrated.* Secretariat made a lot of money for his owner, who had won him in a coin toss with another breeder. She tells the story of how Secretariat was "just a foal with three white feet" when she aquired him. Racing lore claimed that three white feet was a sign a horse would be slow. Secretariat's owner had never believed that legend...clearly, neither did Secretariat!

Horse racing is just as colorful and exciting as auto racing, but there is a lot less noise. Horse racing is often called the "sport of kings." This is partly because buying, training, and keeping horses is a very expensive endeavor.

Horse racing is a breathtaking spectacle. The horses burst out of the gates. "They're off!" shouts the stadium announcer. Amid a thunder of powerful animals and flying dirt, the jockeys lean forward. The crowd's roar increases all the way to the finish line. Sometimes, the race is so close that the winning horse crosses the line only by the length of its nose. Cameras are set up to snap automatically to capture these "photo finishes."

The three biggest races in the United States are the Belmont Stakes, Kentucky Derby, and the

The finish line at the Kentucky Derby

Preakness. These three races make up the annual Triple Crown. Only 11 horses have won all three events. The most recent triple-crown winners were Secretariat (1973), Seattle Slew (1977), and Affirmed (1978). Without a doubt, the brightest jewel in the Triple Crown is the **Kentucky Derby**. The race has been held every year since 1875 at Churchill Downs in Louisville, Kentucky. The race, held on the first Sunday in May, is a beautiful spectacle. Churchill Downs is a graceful, white oval of seating surrounding a perfect grass and red-dirt track. About 130,000 spectators crowd the stands and infield. Louisville celebrates the Derby all day with parties that are both elegant and rowdy. To many Americans, the stately architecture of Churchill Downs and the gala Derby parties are the definition of traditional southern charm and hospitality.

At the beginning of the 20th century, bicycling was a favorite recreation of many Americans.

The **bicycle** first appeared in the late 1700s in Europe. More than a century later, the first U.S. patent for a bicycle was awarded in 1866. Many early bicycles had front wheels that were 5 feet (1.5 m) high! A person riding such a "highwheeler" was perched far above the ground and was at risk of serious accidents. In 1885, an English manufacturer created the "safety bicycle." This version employed a chain and brakes, along with smaller wheels. By 1890, bikes looked much like they do today. By the turn of the century, Americans were in love with the bicycle, and bicycle riding was a favorite pastime for millions of people. The popularity of the bicycle faded with the advent of the automobile in the early 1900s. In the middle of the century, most bike riders were children. But since the 1970s, millions of adults have chosen the bicycle as a means of fun and exercise.

A new kind of racing called **motocross** was created in the United States. This form of motorcycle racing is especially popular among teenagers. Tracks are made of packed dirt and feature bumps and hairpin turns. Riders use protective clothing and helmets. They ride small bikes with wide, knobby tires for traction and control.

Above: American Greg LeMond won the Tour de France three times (1986, 1989, and 1990). The Tour de France is the most famous and challenging bicycle race in the world; it covers about 2,000 miles (3,200 km) and takes three weeks to complete. LeMond was the first American to win the race.

Left: Motocross races are held either outside or on indoor dirt tracks built specifically for the race.

Chapter Five
The Olympics

Across the United States, young athletes wake up early and go to work. A ten-year-old girl wakes up at dawn for gymnastics practice before school. In a sweaty city gym, a teenage boxer absorbs punches, skips rope, and listens attentively to his trainer. A college sprinter studies a computer model of himself in stride. These young men and women share a similar dream: making the U.S. Olympic team.

For most athletes, making the Olympic team is a dream, but winning a gold medal is unimaginable. Many Olympic hopefuls are inspired by stories of U.S. Olympic heroes of the past. There is no greater American sports hero than Jesse Owens.

Above: Jesse Owens, perhaps the greatest American Olympic hero

Opposite page: Bonnie Blair, U.S. Olympic speed skater

Jesse Owens became a legend in the 1936 Summer Olympics, which were held in Berlin, Germany. These Olympic Games were presided over by the German dictator, Adolf Hitler. Hitler believed that white Germans were a "master race" and that Jews and blacks, among others, were inferior. In the coming decade, Hitler led Germany into World War II while murdering millions of innocent people in the Holocaust. In 1936, Hitler hoped the Olympics would be an opportunity to demonstrate German athletes' strength and skill. But an African-American, Jesse Owens, won four track-and-field gold medals. His superb performance proved to the world that Hitler's beliefs of superiority were misguided and wrong.

Jim Thorpe, seen here playing for the Canton Bulldogs foot-ball team in 1921

Another towering legend in U.S. Olympic lore is that of Jim Thorpe. Still renowned as one of the great athletes of the 20th century, Thorpe was an American Indian from Oklahoma. He excelled in many sports, including baseball and football. In the 1912 Olympic Games, he won both the pentathlon and decathlon. The pentathlon is a combination of five different sports, such as swimming and running. The decathlon is considered the ultimate Olympic achievement — ten different track-and-field events involving running, jumping, and throwing.

After the 1912 Olympics, the Olympic Committee discovered that Thorpe had played a few games of professional baseball in 1909 and 1910. They decided that he was a professional athlete, not an amateur. Therefore, he was not eligible for the Olympics. His medals were taken away. Thorpe went on to play major-league baseball from 1913 to 1920. He also helped found the NFL in

1920. Thorpe died in 1953, and 30 years later, the International Olympic Committee returned his two gold medals to his family.

Baron Pierre de Courbertin, a French educator, conceived of the modern Olympics. He believed that sports build character in athletes and could be used to promote world peace. His dream of a world-wide, unifying event was realized in 1896, when the first modern Olympics were held in Athens, Greece. The games were held in Athens because they were based on similar competitions held in ancient Greece two thousand years before.

In the 1980 Winter Olympics, the U.S. hockey team stunned the world by winning a gold medal (above). Throughout the 1980s and 1990s, Florence Griffith Joyner (below), has continued winning Olympic medals and setting records.

1968 and Black Power

In the late 1960s, the civil rights movement gained strength in the United States. It provided the inspiration for one of the most stunning and controversial moments in Olympic history. U.S. sprinters Tommie Smith and John Carlos placed first and third in the 200-meter race. As the two athletes took their places on the medal stand, they shocked the world. Each wore a black glove and black socks without shoes. As "The Star Spangled Banner" was played, Smith and Carlos bowed their heads and each raised a gloved fist in the air.

Carlos later explained that they wore no shoes to represent black poverty. He went on to say that their heads were bowed during the national anthem because the words of the song describe a freedom that existed only for white Americans. Their raised fists were a "black power" sign of the era, which stood for unity and strength among African-Americans.

Since 1896, the Olympics have been canceled only three times — in 1916 because of World War I, and in 1940 and 1944 because of World War II. In many other years, however, political controversies have marred the Olympic Games. In 1980, U.S. president Jimmy Carter did not allow the U.S. team to participate in the summer games that were held in Moscow, the capital of the Soviet Union. Earlier in the year, the Soviets had invaded neighboring Afghanistan. The U.S. government boycotted the games to protest the invasion. President Carter was criticized by many people who maintained that the Olympics should not have been used to make a political statement. Four years later, the Soviets kept their athletes out of the 1984 Summer Olympics at Los Angeles, California.

In the 1980s, the International Olympic Committee began relaxing rules that prevented professional athletes from competing in the Olympics. Immediately, basketball fans in the

United States allowed their imaginations to run wild. Think of it — Magic Johnson passing to Michael Jordan and Larry Bird. Add Patrick Ewing in the middle, with Charles Barkley crashing the boards. Bring such All-Stars as John Stockton, Scottie Pippen, and David Robinson off the bench. It would be a dream.

The Dream Team became a reality at the 1992 Summer Olympic Games in Barcelona, Spain. With the best players from the NBA representing the United States, the rest of the world could hope to win nothing more than the second-place silver medal. The Dream Team lived up to its own hype. They slaughtered opponents by an average of 44 points. Some fans wondered if so many superstars on the same team would lead to bickering over playing time and scoring privileges. But coach Chuck Daly did a brilliant job of managing the stars' egos. Each member of the Dream Team said he was humbled by the experience of winning an Olympic gold medal.

The 1992 Dream Team on the medal stand (left to right): Magic Johnson, Charles Barkley, Chris Mullin, John Stockton, Karl Malone, Clyde Drexler, Michael Jordan, Scottie Pippen, Larry Bird, Patrick Ewing, David Robinson, Christian Laettner.

At the 1976 Olympics, Bruce Jenner (right) won the gold medal in the decathlon, a test of ten different track-and-field events.

At the 1984 Olympics, American Mary Lou Retton (opposite page) won gold medals and the hearts of gymnastics fans around the world.

For nearly two decades, Carl Lewis (below) has proven himself as the greatest track-and-field athlete in the world.

A century of Olympic competition has provided many moments for United States athletes to shine. Mark Spitz captured seven swimming gold medals at the 1972 Summer Olympics, winning every event he entered. At the 1994 Winter Olympics, speed skater Bonnie Blair became the biggest U.S. medal-winner in Olympic history. In the 1984 Olympics, Carl Lewis topped Jesse Owens's feat of 1936, winning gold in the 100-meter and 200-meter races, the long jump, and the men's 4x100-meter relay. Lewis may be the greatest track-and-field star ever. Few humans have ever run the 100-meter race in less than ten seconds. Lewis has done it more than 25 times!

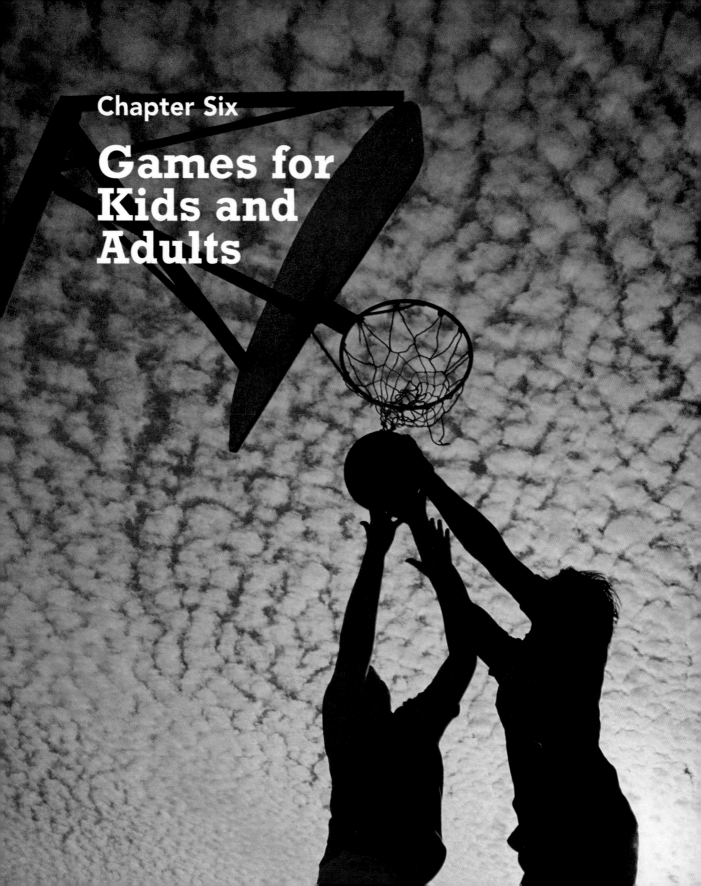

Chapter Six

Games for Kids and Adults

Playing marbles is a longtime favorite sidewalk game of American kids.

A sidewalk is the perfect setting for all sorts of activities. From skateboarding to in-line skating to jogging, millions of American adults and children get their exercise on neighborhood sidewalks. Meanwhile, young children spend many summer hours kneeling on the hot cement playing a variety of different games.

Kids all over the United States play **jacks**, a game that has delighted generations of children. Jacks involves hand-eye coordination. The game requires a bouncy rubber ball and small metal or plastic "jacks." A player bounces the ball and, while it is still in the air, scoops up a specific number of jacks in one hand. Then, just as quickly, the player must catch the ball in his or her other hand before it bounces a second time. The tricks get harder and harder as the game moves along.

Jump rope is another longtime favorite sidewalk game. **Double Dutch** is a more complex version of jump rope. This game uses two ropes instead of one. The turners, who stand at either end of the ropes, are as important as the jumpers. Their job is difficult. They must keep the ropes turning in opposite directions, "egg-beater"

style. They must maintain a constant speed to allow one or more jumpers to perform their tricks. Double Dutchers call out fast-paced rhymes to help keep turners and jumpers in unison. Double Dutch is today a competitive sport. The best teams from all over the country attend the World Championships in a different city each year.

In the 1950s, kids everywhere went crazy for a simple plastic tube. The **hula hoop** was just a large plastic hoop with plastic pellets inside. The pellets added weight and made a swishing sound. Kids kept the hoop swinging around their waist by swiveling their hips. The hula hoop became a craze that was eventually picked up by adults.

Kids playing with hula hoops

Soon, the hula-hoop fad gave way to a brightly colored plastic disk that, when thrown backhand-style, sailed through the air like a flying saucer. An invention of the 1960s, the **Frisbee** is still popular today. Variations on simple Frisbee-tossing games include Frisbee golf and ultimate Frisbee, which is a cross between soccer and football played with the disk. Also, dogs love chasing flying Frisbees and catching them in their mouths.

In the 1980s, the Frisbee was surpassed in popularity by the **hackey sack**. The sack is perhaps the simplest toy to come along in years: a small leather pouch filled with pellets or beans. The hackey sack was invented to be "juggled" by soccer players who stood in a circle and kept it in the air without using their hands. Players may use only their feet, knees, chest, and head to keep a hackey sack in the air. From college campuses to elementary-school playgrounds, millions of young people love playing hackey sack.

Playing hackey sack is a way of juggling with your legs and feet!

When the weather doesn't allow kids to play outside, indoor games take over. Since the 1800s, U.S. inventors have developed some of the world's most popular board games. And, as with many other cultures, chess and checkers are longtime staples of American fun and games.

These traditional games now are being challenged by **computer games**. In the 1970s, a game called Pong became the first video game to gain wide popularity in American homes. Today, Pong (a simple, black-and-white paddle game) would seem boring compared to the elaborate, animated video games that are available. With modern computer technology, players can "do" anything — from playing basketball against Shaquille O'Neal to solving complicated murder mysteries. The next generation of

Monopoly was invented during the Great Depression, which began in 1929. In that time of economic strife, few people had enough money to own property, let alone feed their families. Monopoly allowed people to fantasize about owning properties, building houses and hotels, and charging rent.

Computer games range from those that run on a personal computer or television (left) to the exciting world of virtual reality (below).

computer games involves virtual reality. In these games, players go "inside" the computer for a thrilling 3-D experience.

Technology is revolutionizing recreation in the United States. In the late 20th century, millions of people spend much of their free time sitting at personal computers or watching television. Physicians worry that electronic entertainment lures too many people away from the physical exercise involved in traditional sports and games. But even in this electronic age, sports such as basketball and soccer are wildly popular among Americans, young and old.

lossary

aerobic
exercises or sports that increase the body's respiration and heart rate

amateur
one who performs a service (or plays a sport) without being paid money

ballpark
a baseball stadium or field

boycott
to purposely avoid doing business with an individual, group, or company

fad
an activity or clothing style that suddenly achieves tremendous popularity

foal
a horse under one year old

gentleman's agreement
unwritten understanding guaranteed by only a spoken pledge or a secret promise

gymnastics
several exercises in which athletes perform acrobatic feats of balancing, jumping, and flipping

hole in one
a golf shot in which a player places the ball in the cup with just one swing

hurdle
barrier over which a runner must jump in track-and-field

induction
formal ceremony in which a person is admitted into a group or institution, such as a Hall of Fame

industry
a group of businesses related to the same product or products; the "sports industry" involves all of the money-making businesses connected to sports

jockey
a person who rides a racehorse

knockout
boxing victory achieved when one's opponent loses consciousness

major leagues
the top professional U.S. baseball leagues; the American League and the National League

medal stand
a platform upon which athletes stand to receive their awards after winning a competition

methanol
liquid alcohol that is commonly used in auto racing as a safer alternative to gasoline

Muslim
a follower of the
Islamic religion

Negro Leagues
pro baseball leagues in the
early 1900s in which African-
Americans and Latinos played
because they were not
allowed into the all-white
major leagues

pastime
an entertainment, game,
or sport

patent
an official document recogniz-
ing that a person has invented
an object, machine, or concept

prize fight
a boxing match
with an important
award or title at stake

professional
one who is paid money to
perform a service (or play
a sport)

royalty
a privileged, wealthy class in
society; families related to a
king or queen

thrill sports
activities that place one in
danger of injury (such as
bungee jumping or sky
surfing)

track-and-field
a group of sports events
involving running, jumping,
and throwing (such as timed
running races, high jump, long
jump, shot put, and javelin)

traction
the force that holds an object
to a surface (such as a tire to
pavement)

wind resistance
the force that wind exerts
against an object that is
moving through the air

YMCA
Young Men's Christian
Association; an organization
that promotes young people's
spiritual and physical well-
being

For Further Reference

Books

Ashe, Arthur. *A Hard Road to Glory: A History of African-American Athletes.* New York: Armistad, 1993.

Diamond, Dan. *The Official NHL 75th Anniversary Commemorative Book.* Toronto: Firefly Books, 1991.

Feineman, Neal. *Wheel Excitement: The Official Rollerblade Guide to In-Line Skating.* New York: Hearst Books, 1991.

McDonough, Will. *75 Seasons: The Complete Story of the NFL.* Atlanta: Turner Publications, 1995.

McKissack, Frederick & Patricia. *Black Diamond: The Story of the Negro Baseball Leagues.* New York: Scholastic, 1994.

Nelson, Kevin. *Pickle Pepper and Tip-In, Too: 250 Games and Activities for Kids.* New York: Fireside, 1994.

Packer, Billy and Roland Lazenbury. *The Golden Game.* Dallas: Taylor Publishing, 1991.

Siddons, Larry (Ed.). *The Olympics at 100.* New York: Macmillan, 1995.

Stewart, Peter. *Way to Play: Soccer.* Rocklin, CA: Carlton Books, 1995.

Organizations

Amateur Athletic Union of the United States, 3400 W. 86th Street, Indianapolis, IN 46268

American Fitness Association, 6285 E. Spring Street, #404, Long Beach, CA 90808

International Professional Rodeo Association, 2304 Exchange Ave, P.O. Box 8377, Oklahoma City, OK 73108

International Soap Box Derby, P.O. Box 7233, Akron, OH 44306

Little League Baseball, Inc., PO Box 3485, Williamsport, PA 17701

National Collegiate Athletic Association (NCAA), 6201 College Boulevard, Overland Park, KS 66211

United States Olympic Committee, 1 Olympic Plaza, Colorado Springs, CO 80909

United States Soccer Federation, 1801-1811 S. Prairie Avenue, Chicago, IL 60616

Halls of Fame

International Tennis Hall of Fame, 194 Bellevue Avenue, Newport, RI 02840

Naismith Memorial Basketball Hall of Fame, 1150 W. Columbus Avenue, Springfield, MA 01101

National Baseball Hall of Fame & Museum, PO Box 590, Cooperstown, NY 13326

National Boxing Hall of Fame, 1 Hall of Fame Drive, Canastota, NY 13032

National Track & Field Hall of Fame, 1 RCA Dome, Suite 140, Indianapolis, IN 46225

Professional Football Hall of Fame, 2121 George Halas Drive NW, Canton, OH 44708

Professional Hockey Hall of Fame, 30 Young Street BCE Place, Toronto, Ontario, Canada M5E 1X8

Index

Photo Credits

Cover photograph copyright ©: Sports Photo Masters, Inc. (Vincent S. Gogluicci)

Photographs copyright ©: AP/Wide World Photos: pp. 1 top, 26, 46, 49 bottom, 50, 52 top, 57 top; Sports Photo Masters, Inc.: pp. 1 bottom left, 20, 53 (all Mitchell B. Reibel), 14 (Noren Trotman), 16 (David L. Greene), 54 (Robert J. Rodgers); Tony Stone Images: pp. 1 bottom right, 35 bottom right (both Lori Adamski Peek), 58 (Frank Herholdt); PhotoEdit: pp. 2–3, 56 (all Robert Brenner), 55, 58 bottom (Tony Freeman), 59 top (David Young-Wolff); National Baseball Library & Archives, Cooperstown, NY: pp. 4, 6, 7, 8; UPI/Bettmann: pp. 5, 9 top, 17, 24, 29, 41, 42, 43, 48; Reuters/Bettmann: pp. 12, 45 top right; The Bettmann Archive: p. 44; Lloyd Fox: p. 9 bottom; North Wind Picture Archives: p. 10; Comstock: pp. 13, 21 top left; Naismith Memorial Basketball Hall of Fame: p. 15 (both); Gamma Liaison International: pp. 19 bottom (John David Fleck), 27 (Art Seitz); Allsport: pp. 21 bottom right, 28 (J. D. Cuban), 30 (Simon Bruty), 38 (Steve Swope), 47, 49 top (Steve Powell), 51 (Mike Powell), 52 bottom (David Connon); Bruce Bennet Studios: pp. 22, 23 (both Bruce Bennet); Sports Chrome Inc.: pp. 31 (Rene Robert), 33 (Brian Drake), 35 top, 37 (Kim Stallknecht), 40 top, 45 bottom left (Brian Drake); J. H. Peterson: p. 32; F-Stock Inc.: p. 34 (Jeffrey S. Boucher); IMS Photo: p. 39 (Lance Sellers); Don Garlitts Museum of Drag Racing: p. 40 bottom; *The Palm Beach Post*: p. 59 bottom (Bob Shanley).

About the Author

Philip Brooks grew up near Chicago and now lives in Columbus, Ohio, with his wife, Balinda Craig-Quijada. He attended the University of Iowa Writers' Workshop, where he received an M.F.A. in fiction writing. His stories have appeared in a number of literary magazines, and he has written several books for children. He is the author of *Michael Jordan: Beyond Air* and *Dikembe Mutombo: Mount Mutombo* (Children's Press), and the Franklin Watts First Books *Georgia O'Keeffe* and *Mary Cassatt*.

BOOKMOBILE

GAYLORD F